LESSER SPOTTED

LESSER SPOTTED

SANDRA BUNTING

Gaelóg Press

Published by Gaelóg Press, Canada, 2023
First Electronic Edition by Gaelóg Press, Canada, 2023

Gaelóg Press
Sandra Bunting, editor
409 Burnt Church Rd.
Burnt Church, New Brunswick,
Canada E9G4C9

ISBN 978-1-9994618-1-2

Cover Image: @Chrisp543/Dreamstime.com

Book design by Cyberscribe.eu

In appreciation to Gisèle LeBlanc and Bob Skillen
for all their support
and in giving me a nurturing space in which to work.

TABLE OF CONTENTS

RETURN FLIGHT/ AS THE CROW FLIES 109

THE NEST

TRANSITION TO SUMMER

They enter like strange flora,
cotton T-shirts of summer fruit,
hair plaited in rainbow rubber bands,
loose strands escaping baseball hats.

The stylish teacher says in French
they can each choose two books
and they answer back in languages
as different as the colours of their skin.

They do not know the library
is named after a beautiful poet
or that the librarian never wants
to go home to Bulgaria again

but in straight lines at the door
two books under their arms,
they sense the heart of the person
reading in the corner is bleeding.

The door opens to a summer breeze,
the black and white day is coloured in
with melted crayons from their pockets,
only sometimes going outside the lines.

ORIGAMI WITH DAUGHTERS

We find a private area, a bench to sit
to fold paper squares into delicate birds.
In Japan it's good luck to make cranes,
hang them together in long strings,
pull their patterned wings up and down,
hold their fragile life gently in your hand.

Twenty-five paper shapes wait beside us,
wanting to come to life, almost ready to fly,
outside gulls soar and screech into the wind,
oily cormorants splash after fish as they dive,
a heron walks past the window, as if he
were an experiment, one we made before.

HOUSE OF DAUGHTERS

The days dragging her
twenty miles to watch
a GAA match in the rain,

or her feigned interest
in rugby strategy while
secretly sending texts,

Barbies in her backpack, she
jumps in alarm at the clamour,
a soccer goal scored
but
it dwindles in importance
when she comes home with Kafka,
Sartre and Proust in her pocket

and he knows she is ready
to stay up conversing
'til three in the morning

while he digs out his old books,
tries to remember the lines,
relives his teenage angst

only to be taken by surprise
when she brings home a boy
who asks the score of the match.

FRAGMENTS

I admit I've kept things from you,
packed them away
where you could not find them.
I fed you bits, crumbling the rest,
dry leaves in my hand,
to keep you in the dark,
shield you from the battles
and meanness of my age.

What harm to think we come
from a line of kings?
How far back do we have to go
to dislodge secrets of the past?
Can we ever know?

Now you say you have
to find where you come from,
know me to understand yourself,
I become the answer
to your questions
but still scramble to piece
together the slivers of the past.

THE REBEL

Dublin

There is no one among men that has not a special failing.   Po Chu I

Stuffed back in a corner
of Matt Browne's bookshop,
long-haired and fresh-cheeked,
he loses himself
amongst multi-coloured books.

He watches the clock
'til the slender-pointed
shadow passes the hour,
lunchtime finished.

Distance then spreads out
from priests and rugby games,
from the Blackrock College
big gates and tailored lawns.

He rises, pockets Proust,
and strides quickly out
through clumps of dirty

slush turning to puddles
to find another corner
into which to curl, and let
the Frenchman draw him in.

SECRETS

Miramichi, Canada

It was not my intention to let you go,
so when you stepped off the plane
from Dublin in your light jacket
and summer shoes and felt the heat
of sun on your face, autumn leaves
blazing scarlet, orange, and gold,
I let you enjoy it, kept the bite
of winter to myself but hid a supply
of heavy socks and long underwear
under the bed to keep you warm.

An artist in Saskatchewan is calling
for people to tell her their secrets,
she is putting them inside pages
of books she has carved out,
leaving them randomly, secretly
in public libraries across Canada,
what book would contain my secret,
in what town would mine end up?

DENDROPHOBIA*

Although you feared them at first,
the trees pulled you in,
their spirit enveloped softly around
like pine needles on moss.
Stars, close to the earth,
filled a black sky so immense
that you couldn't help but feel part of it.
Then at the Irish festival
in a skating rink in summer disuse,
you were coaxed to recite a poem.
You performed *Donal Óg* by heart,
(translation from the Irish)
to wild acclaim and applause.
The reward - a pitcher of green beer,
strange acts, all part of settling in.

* Fear of Trees

TREE WALK

When we lived in my land,
I told you the names of trees,
as we trudged through snow
on the hunt for pussy willows,
heads filled with spruce scent.

At night I whispered
the names to you
like a prayer.

You didn't know the names
of trees in your land.
Barren hills rising from the sea
fooled me into thinking there were none
but I rooted them out in the end,
found them ancient and wise.

I shouted out names of trees to you,
words picked up on my walks.
You let them put their branches
around you, nourish you,
give strength, absorbing you.
You put words to lullabies,
gave voice to our entwined lives.

FIDDLER FOG

My mother's hair grew in after
chemo, the colour now changed
from strawberry blond to salt and pepper.
When the dog arrived at eight weeks old
with her grey coat and black face,
she claimed it as her baby.

I was in love. The tiny terrier jumped
in the bath, swam round my dear one.
It sunk beneath the snow in winter,
cold hard clumps sticking to its fur
and melting in puddles. It warmed
itself between our chests as we kissed.

FOGGY DEW

You loved everyone but old men
which you'd pin against the wall.
You herded swans three times bigger
than yourself into the sea,
and you herded us,
tried to keep us together,
wouldn't let us stray behind,
checked to see if anyone was missing
until we found we were missing you.

OLD CATS

After an absence I return
to discover the passing away
of several old cats of my acquaintance,
missing parts of the landscape now
at the homes of different friends.

I thought they'd never disappear
but go they did, and the names
Sultana and *Georgie* won't be called
and I'll not be asked to mind them
again when their owners go away.

Even old dogs are getting older,
parts not working as they used to,
and I sense a quivering in the air
as if my ghostly terrier is near,
digging up flowers at the university,
chasing blowing leaves, and old cats.

AIR CURRENTS

UNDER A NORWEGIAN SUN

after Edvard Munch's *The Sun*

No ghost walks here,
only us tall under the sun.
Warming.
Snow in woods, dirty now,
shrinks into Nordic shadows.

And everything is the sun,
a wooden hut through trees,
a book dropped in a mountain stream,
trolls disguised as nature,
your overstuffed handbag,
your disappearing suitcase.
Warming.

In the north colours swirl,
clear air moves south,
the body a small cyclone
of brightness.
Warming.

Squirrels chatter
snip snap snuter
and under this midnight sun,
I can never get warm.

A HIGH OF MINUS TWELVE

Ice under boots, you walk snowy streets
to a row of houses and knock at a door,
Leonard Cohen invites you into his pain.

Shadows deepen the park to a bluish tone,
childish voices slide from the mountain,
sun dances on a solitary skater.

Waiting like a sparrow under darkness of a hawk,
the unknown darts out of the corner of your eye,
something you thought was real, was not.

Yes, those black dots run after you
leap in the air and they finally get you
but not in the form you thought they would.

Hundreds of pigeons, feathers puffed,
warm themselves on heating vents
under icicles, cold daggers to the heart.

BLACK BEARS

The bears in my head have come out of hibernation,
drawn out by a few days of sunshine and small buds.
Five more weeks to coax out spring. By then the bears
are starving, reluctant epicures of small insects and frogs.
A prolific year, the long-legged cubs lope, curious,
inside the spring allergy-filled emptiness of my skull.
In soft figure-eight winds, a robin lands heralding spring
only to retreat when ice forms again in puddles,
snowflakes tumble, and hail rains in a chilled blue sky.

It is summer now and the bears sit in my garden
under the apple tree at the side of the house
and wander back to raspberries, and black currants.
A man with emphysema runs three fields
from a snorting mother until he gasps for breath,
not noticing the bear has long ago given up the chase.
They don't try to get inside so I don't see them
but friends keep away, joggers speed past.

In the age of nowhere to roam, bears
have found a home inside my cavernous mind,
and get fat, cozy into dry leaves, drift down
to sleep where they are welcome 'til spring again.

MY MAZE

I am sometimes away with crows
in high trees back of Aula Maxima.
They pick at twigs of dreams,
weave stories deep in their nests,
scatter them low on the chestnut walk.

Ravens swoop at a pizza delivery man
unfortunate enough to find one dead,
and they, thinking he is to blame, attack,
armies of magpies, jackdaws, and rooks.
They know. They know. But have it wrong.

And one lone seagull dives at a dog,
too big now to lift high into the air,
though the bird still lunges on cue, a game,
it glides over ducks and coots on the canal,
dodging the cloud-like wings of swans.

The American girl, who studied at McGill,
delighted in melodious birdsong at night,
the same music that wound itself
through bare trees as I left you
at the gates each night in the fading light.

This is the maze I have created,
crows, never far away, caw, caw, cawing
a warning that it is of my design,
I am too late, like this year's cuckoo
with no nest to leave its eggs.

AUSPICY

STANDING AT CARNAC

On viewing prehistoric standing stones in Brittany

We've become stones in a field
solidly planted in a seafaring land,
standing for such a long time we've
forgotten what we're supposed to do.

Are we clues to ancient mysteries,
or signs of future wonders? I don't know.
I only remember the old days when I
used to dance and make eyes at the one,
'Le geant', our child laughing by the fire.

We hunted well, were good gatherers,
loved when the sun went down,
made the Gods lonely because of that.

And now we stand.

I have watched women dancing
in their velvet robes and lace coifs
and try to join in. And yet stand still.
Even trees have more movement,
can feel the wind rustle their leaves
let themselves sway to its music.

I refuse to believe it is a punishment.
Though hard, the world and its beauty
renews our happiness every day.
I prefer to think we have a purpose,
protecting, perhaps, this one green world
until all danger has passed and we can
dance, dance, dance, dance again.

A SHOUT FROM DOWNSTAIRS

More often than not the call
was about something I'd done wrong,
the burning pot left on the stove
or wet snow tracked though the overheated
kitchen from the great outdoors.

It came, at times, from what I'd
neglected to do to get though winter:
shovel a path, chop ice from the steps,
buy red wine, make reservations
for a sunshine holiday in February.

Or, in summer, it could be an expression
of desperation at not finding insect repellent,
ravenous mosquitoes waiting to devour,
clean socks, keys and glasses always missing,
along with my mind that was here a minute ago.

The middle of last winter the call was a whisper,
a crow's warning when you told me your bad news
and the world shrunk away from us.
On the city sidewalk we fought back tears,
traffic noise blotted out, passing people invisible.

But, in spring, the call was a baby moose
stopping in our yard to enjoy the morning dew,
gangly yet proud in its own particular beauty
before it ambled towards woods to wade in water
and the sun rose deep orange as we held hands.

TIDE

It comes in quickly.
There is no time
to run back to shore.

In Doolin many years ago,
a baby in my arms,
it sneaked up on me.
Against the current
you pulled us out,
dangerous to stare too long
at the reddening sunset.

And just last weekend
absorbed in collecting shells
on the little coral beach
of Lettermullen,
we found ourselves cut off,
stranded on seaweed-covered rocks.

You, with your wellies, carried
me to safety on your back,
coaxed the dog to swim across,
the pile of shells left behind.

You find yourself on a beach,
the swift tide coming in
causing me to go to sea every day,
practise my strokes
so I can swim under water
to tug you back to dry land.

KEEPSAKE

September 08, Montreal

I was surprised when you,
who do not keep things,
picked up a chestnut
outside the gates of McGill.

It is in your pocket even now
after you were hollowed on one side
and you still consider it
your good luck charm.

FIRST TIME

We were given a room with a view,
overlooking city skyscrapers where
on tiptoes we could see the St. Lawrence
and small mountains at the border.

The blinds were pulled back
letting in rays of sunshine,
outside seagulls glided above the clouds,
sky blue brought peace.

While I wondered if I would get vertigo
on one of the roof gardens in sight,
you lay down with a smile and kissed me
before you put your earphones on.

I watched you, in the black shirt I liked,
eyes closed, toes twitching to the music,
I held my breath as poison dripped into you,
an attempt to save you, to save your life.

HY-BRAZIL *

The island glitters
in the middle of the ocean,
an arcane city
built on a living form
submerged at the deepest
part of the Atlantic,
a green star flickering,
only to vanish and reappear
somewhere else.

I have seen
its other side,
the dark side.
It moves along the ocean bed,
occasionally
coming up for air.

When you are pregnant,
so is every other woman
you see, or so it seems,
when someone you love
is afflicted, you see pain
everywhere.

* a mythical Celtic island shrouded in mist, that appears and disappears,
said to be located somewhere off the coast from Galway

IN-BETWEEN LAND

I held your hand along Madrid streets,
told you stories, opened the lock.
The dog is waiting to go for a walk.

Forbidden absinthe was such a treat,
It made me feel like an ancient *Ard-Rí,**
so sad, but then again, so happy.

Hands on my chest to feel the beat,
so difficult to finally part,
you and that place entered my heart.

I imagine so many good things to eat,
sometimes as if I'm in a trance.
Why do I think I am in France?

Roads flooded, tall trees creak,
wind engages in a savage dance.
Why do I think I am in France?

It was a seaweedy beach, rocky and bleak,
mosquitoes biting before you could start,
yet you and that place entered my heart.

Trees and the treeless lands to seek
where wind is calling, calling out to me,
so sad because I am so happy.

I had hoped to stay another week,
enjoying every minute of the bedside talk
but the dog is waiting to go for a walk.

* high king

THIN RESURRECTION

The squirrel I thought was a baby
is a shrunken version of the one
I used to feed last autumn.
It is leaner and its tail scragglier
but it scratches its ear the same way,
still strikes a pose in return for nuts
and looks as if it knows me.

When snow finally melted
after one of the hardest winters
in more than three decades,
the squirrel and a mate materialized
from the tomb in the back garden,
a flaking outdoor storage cupboard,
as if reborn into the fat of the earth.

WIND HOVERING

LOST BIRDS

Galway is the city of many characters including this one

He crouches,
hidden away in bushes,
and before he's visible,
I hear the song,
whistle and twitter
formed by lips
practiced
in the art of music.

No feathers warm
his balding head,
exposed and public.

On weekends,
he plays the old tunes,
goes back to
his piano-playing days,
says we're not ready
for his new voice.

LESSER SPOTTED

*The Snow Bunting is a finch-like bird
with unmusical but distinctive songs.*

Pity to have
the name of a bird
and not to fly.

Me, a poor thing,
small against clouds,
exposed to all eyes-
in the spread of sky,
with a discordant
love song.

Oh to flap my wings
and soar
to the highest rooftop

to search for a perch,
the one true note and
the company of trees!

RECYCLING

Benevista, Spain

Dolores brushes her hair every day
at a table in the back garden
under the lemon tree beside the
avocado plant she started from scratch.

A docile breeze carries fragrance
from rosemary and lavender bushes,
palm trees dance in the distance,
a soft blue haze hovers over the sea.

Dolores' hair bleaches with southern sun,
leaves a blonde tangle in her brush
which she picks out and throws
to nestle among the clover and grass,

attracting the starlings who swoop
up the harvest to reinforce their nests
snugly built on chimney tops,
like turrets of a Mediterranean castle.

Small joys of the natural world, often
unnoticed, the contented lizard basking
on a stone in the sun, Dolores there,
the door wide open, hair blowing.

GOLDEN SONG

You dream of the washing machine
you saved up ten years to buy
then moved to your parents' house
in the country for safekeeping
but the machine was not safe,
your parents were not safe.

You start over in a different house,
with a new washing machine,
a baby girl and a smiling wife
who walks home from the shops
in the cold, snowflakes drifting,
with a bag full of pomegranates
that fall out, split open,
stain the snow like blood.

It's a pile of rubble on Google maps,
yet you dream of your old home,
the room you sat in to have coffee
in the company of 300 singing canaries,
bright feathers catching the sun.

What sound accompanies you now?
The silence of a balsam forest,
a solitary crow flying low, warning,
and the washing machine
always spinning, spinning away.

LILY ROSE *

Bald except for a rose coloured
tuft on the top of her head
she seeks the morning sounds
of crows and jay,
spots the dash of blue and black
dart from branch to branch
bruising the sky,
language familiar yet alien.

She's bad, she bites hard,
enough to pierce your ears
or digs and scratches into your hair,
grooming, a painful massage.

She's bad but likes to play,
her exposed head and body
popping up from a nest of blankets,
practising her dance steps,
back and forth, up and down,
finishing with her signature bite.

* *A rose-crowned conure (parrot)*

FLOCK MEMORY

Irish Border Counties

Perhaps it would not create such horror
if the old myths were never passed down,
if the daffodils had never bloomed
if the fields were not at their greenest,
if lambing season wasn't about to begin.

Who will there be to teach the lambs
the way of the mountains, to train
their tiny hooves along the trail,
pull them towards the light,
through the dips in the hard rock,
up the winding track
to the scent of grass, air pure and moist?

Many ages of sheep
caution and guide
to navigate well worn paths,
beaten down from generations,
to let the lambs learn the hills,
and leap for joy
at their precious gift of life.

* *With the breakout of the highly contagious Foot and Mouth disease in
the border counties of Ireland several years ago, whole flocks of sheep had
to be destroyed.*

DANCE FOR STONES

Connemara

Leenane in lambing season,
the curve of a river through green fields,
sheep with muddy wool and tired eyes
watch the energetic young step lightly.

You have become firm, silent,
a keen observer of weather,
present inside these stones,
the rough hills of Connemara.

Clouds that melt in your mouth
descend, darken, and eat tops of hills,
absorbing them into mist,
dissolving into rain on all below.

Rain on the bent whitethorn,
rain on oaks, hazels, and grassy rings,
wind whipping around stone,
unsettling loughs, holy places, and the sea.

High up sight-stones and song-stones,
music if we can find the key,
the echo of accordion on land below,
a few steps on slate in the old way.

Back to the city of water and of stone,
past the Crane pub on the corner
to a shelf in a stone house, a little pile
of coloured stones in your memory there.

MIGRATION

UNDER THE JURAS

Cern Experiments

It has rained non-stop since I have returned,
feathery branches of trees shake with wind,

sending horse chestnuts to the ground, small this year,
not good enough to use as autumn conkers.

Images of Cuba splash onto a screen at the gym,
mesmerising effect of a downgraded hurricane.

Waves as big as houses smash the Malecón,
pastel villages sit silent and surreal under water.

The sea throws up particles onto the Isla
and on this island of Ireland, we're drowning too.

We decide our future, lead our quiet lives,
or get sucked deep into that black hole,

absolutely nothing to split atoms about,
aren't we all particles of God? Stardust.

NEW BOOTS FOR WARSAW

Nowy Buty dla Warsawy

Peacocks in Lazienki park
are Polish, born in Warsaw,
accustomed now to cold,
their footprints leave evidence
of a complex dance in snow,
winter performers on the deserted
amphitheater to an audience
of wind-swept leaves.

Squirrels hurry in front of them,
courtly pages announcing
their presence at the old palace,
rebuilt like almost everything
in Warsaw after it was burnt
in the war. Peacocks screech
at red foxes from the safety
of a roof where they sleep at night.

I found some peace here
among piles of dead leaves
and bare-branched trees,
shuffling around Chopin's monument

the scent of dry roses,
strains of a Polonaise showing the way
to the church entombed
in the crisp autumn air that holds his heart.

MIRACLES IN CZESTOCHOWA

What can you do for me,
Black Madonna
with your gaunt face, sad eyes,
what can you do for me
who has everything,
no crippled limbs,
no twisted fingers,
no poison in my blood,
no intrusive cells,
no extreme loss?

What can you do for me?
How can I ask you to fill
this silly disquiet inside?

I would add what jewels I have
to those on your gilded walls
to feel a sense of peace in my head,
but feel humbled
by what I see around me,
signs of suffering crammed
into every available space,
crutches, molds of body parts.
I avert my eyes from the afflicted.

A shift in the eye
in the direction of the child,
seems to say to me –
you who has
everything,
be thankful,
take good care
of what you have.

COMING HOME

A Visit to Auschwitz

I stand in snow,
drawn into the graveyard
of southern Poland
covered by whiteness and time.

Yet roots like bones prod,
ashes shape barren trees,
dust brick buildings
and settle like silt in the lakes.

With frozen fingers,
I brush away something
that lodges in my hair.
I make a snowball,
but even in sunshine,
it seems inappropriate.
I drop it along the path
outside Number 10.

A long wait at the airport,
time for heavy thoughts.

A final landing in Galway
to unseasonable snowflakes
then at my door,
smiles from those I love,
a little dog jumping at my feet.

STEALING STORIES

Strong winds scatter leaves across the fields,
those from my trees gather in piles on my neighbour's lawn,
he rakes them into a ditch, not noticing the intruders,
sets fire to them, lets them burn until they crumple into ash.

The same with acorns. Squirrels pick them up
from under his oak tree and drop them on my lawn,
I treasure them, put them in a place of honour
on my windowsill to reflect on and be inspired.

We all have our own stories to tell, good or bad,
tales connect living things: trees, animals, us,
and words crisscross, weaving through the air
touching us deeply, making us want to retell the tale.

We can understand each other better if we share,
what we bring to each other breaks down walls,
our narratives chip away at discord, embrace
each other and enrich the only world we have.

ENOUGH

Two amateur philosophers,
one at the back of the queue,
the other wise man serving
at the Galway Saturday Market:

— *Any Moroccan olives left?*
— *There are enough.*
— *Yes, but what is enough?*

On the Mosquito Coast
you ate what you got
no second helpings;
one plate,
one cup of coffee
and even if you craved more,
it never came.

So after my third latte
at a Galway café,
still not satisfied,
I could almost taste
the single cup in Raista
feel how it cradled
warm in my hands

as I sat on the porch
of a straw-roofed hut,
in out of the storm,
the crack of thunder,
punctuation of lightning.

BANANA RIVER

Mosquito Coast, Honduras

Let God into your heart,
said a Mosquito Coast native
in bad Spanish.
Cornered by non-stop talk
of a god we no longer believed in,
we finally paid for her
to get into a canoe
and take her word
to the next village.
Looking back she cried
that those with fear
in their hearts could not enter
the kingdom of heaven.

Later dipping my toe
into the Rio Platano
I thought about the fear
I got from my father,
from my mother, my cautious life
and into a river where crocodiles lurk

I plunged, allowing myself
to be swept down by the current,
discovering play, trusting myself
to swim back upstream.

LURE OF VOLCANO

After Malcolm Lowry

You did it to yourself,
walked too close to volcanoes,
ended up like the mangy dog
you used to kick
when you were someone else,
the same old faded posters
of disaster films in Spanish
haunting your head.

I didn't make it up Pacaya,
stayed instead in Antiqua,
drinking wine and speaking Spanish.
Still, I felt the hot lava
under my feet melting my shoes.
I knew all the danger signs,
PELIGRO – but went ahead
and bathed in the luxuriant,
destructive heat of red.

TALKING TO THE GODS

The music of Mayan languages:
quiché, cakchquel, k'ekchi, tz'utijil,
jacaltel, achi, jacalteko, akateko,
sounds forming like smoke into the sky,
like flames on a torch, fire at night.

We trekked through places
that were their names:
Chichicastenango, Huehuetenango
Quetzaltenango (place of the quetzal)
and stopped in Panajachel
to use the internet,
our words drifting into the air,
crossing seas in an instant.

Smoke rose in ancient Mayan temples
to communicate with the Gods
the incense of devotion wafting
to make sense of a world
as unpredictable as molten rock,
as cruel as hunger and as war.

We appease a dangerous deity,
the one on high gobbles up

the sentence on the screen,
we press a button and send
our own sacred words down the line,
offerings to a different god.

FIRES OF BELIZE

Like a spider starting a web again
after it was swept away,
people living here would gather bits
of wood and begin to rebuild a house,
knowing that in the pine savannah
nothing is permanent.

Life depends on the fiery whims
of the land where flames appear
in spontaneous combustion.
The families have nowhere else
to go perhaps, or have made this
unwanted land theirs, call it home.

DANCE OF THE FIRE ANTS

Pech Country, Honduras

They took me by surprise
one day in the jungle
while I was sheltering
from tropical rain
under an umbrella-like leaf.

More a march than a dance,
a sense of purpose kept them
in a line along set paths,
bearing burdens into sand mounds,
their underground home.

I felt them before I saw them,
tiny explosions going off on my skin
a whole army moving
from leaf, up my arm,
down my back,
stinging in symmetry.

SIDE BY SIDE

Ancient Mayans would tie an enemy
tightly to the trunk of the poisonwood tree
let the sap run hot and sticky
and mix with the blood of the prisoner.

Even a light brush
made a person writhe in pain,
drove them to dementia.

So close but so hard to reach, an antidote
resting nearby in the branches of a rusty trunked tree:
a symbiotic relationship like dock leaves and nettles.

UNDERWATER DIVERS

Utila, Honduras

They would be wild
if they weren't divers.
They'd be tough as nails,
good in interrogations
or lost in the jungle
eating leaves and maggots
with an unknown tribe.

They discover play
on the floor of the ocean,
swimming round a giant tortoise,
flitting over colourful creatures,
having a manicure by shrimp.

They jump through underwater hoops,
blow bubbles like smoke rings
to the surface of the sea.

They would be wild,
all have had a past,
come from all corners
of the earth
to speak the language
of the depths.

MURMURATION

NORA BARNACLE

The fact that she did what she did
was the butterfly's wing to start the storm,
energy to walk through a Dublin day in June,
material to shape a life away together.

It took a Galway girl to do what she did,
to run off with a man to foreign parts,
not minding what people thought,
the Galway phrase: *I'm not bothered.*

She had to make a man out of him
feed him stories of experience
lived out in back lanes in the west
secretly along canals, near the river.

And because she put up with him,
he persevered to write his great book,
later acclaimed but at first causing uproar
as he leaned on his ash stick, and on Nora.

COLOURS

For Edith

Synesthesia is a rare condition in which a stimulus in one sense is involuntarily elicited in another sense. For instance, someone may be able to hear colours, see sounds or taste shapes.

Confused as a child as to why no one else
saw things as you did, letters and names
fashioned into strange combinations,
smells and tastes taking shape in different hues,
some to be avoided like the tall cold blue
glass that could never be drunk from.

You know the code to the lock,
numbers in the form of colours
that only you can see,
a condition you share with
artists, scientists, and musicians,
with different sensory connections,
in good company, not the only one.

How astonishing it is to know
a number is the colour of old gold,
a certain letter is a shade of faded dung,

and such a word is cornflower blue!
I asked what colour came up
when you thought of my name.
It was silver like tiny bells.

Your red hair, your green scarf,
your pink hat, your purple gloves
and all the colours of the world
swirling in your head, flying out
attaching themselves to
numbers, letters, and words
in their own poetic spectrum.

PHOTOGRAPH WITH HOOKER

A hooker is a traditional Galway sailing craft

for Evelyne

This place called Galway
has other names, sea names, secret names.
It beckoned to us many years ago,
then turned us into familiar figures,
our laughs like those of *cailleacha gránna* *,
a glass of red in our hands
that came, no doubt, in olden days
off some boat at the Spanish arch.

This city has been our home.
Pulled by the force of its current,
we have danced together on waves,
let dogs lead us into hidden paths.
Tearful to leave, but life has its own plan,
I go back to my trees, le grand *fleuve*,
you journey to a stronger *blas*.**

We pose now in front of a camera
in the Galway City Museum, the whale of
a *Ceathrú Rua* hooker*** suspended behind us,

faces of two old friends in Galway
our souls held here forever
by the music at the Crane, launches at galleries,
hedgehogs in the garden among snails.

INSIDE OUTSIDE

Galway City Museum

We are passing clouds that watch
time churn up Galway flotsam,
little pearls scooped in an oyster shell,
scattered within walls to find a place,
always selecting, shaping our stories.

Time scrapes the muddy bottom
of the river where our thoughts form.
Everything changes and remains the same.
In from the bay voices blow. Window
panes dissolve like barley sugar in the rain.

Ghosts whisper messages from the past,
our footsteps heavy on smooth stone
reach out for pebbles from a common pool.
Time shifts again, comes together
to let the light in – let in the light.

PAINTING IN THE DOG

after a painting by Miles Lowry, Annaghmakerrig

The artist sets up his easel deep among trees,
poised to capture velvet in green,
shadows spread on Japanese paper,
the play of light and dark through trunks.

Eyes half closed he examines veined leaves,
looks closer at marks and knots on bark,
straight and still as if he were himself a tree,
he listens to a blackbird's forest melody.

Across the lake a solitary fisherman rows
beneath a hill where deer feed in morning,
on this side a figure walks along the road,
small, in Victorian cape and black bonnet.

She's often seen in the kitchen garden
by the fish pool with newts and tadpoles,
or strolling down by the grey water,
briskly taking in the leaf-green air.

The artist places her among paper trees,
imagines her cane and solemn face,
then finishing the rest from memory,
invites locals to see over glasses of wine.

So, you saw Miss W on her morning trek,
but where's the terrier, her constant friend?
Phantoms together in garden and woods,
pattering on the stairs, routing in the pantry.

Is it down to lethargy or expense?
Miss W will walk and walk until her remains
can lay under the faraway soil of England,
although for years these Irish fields were home.

On textured canvas the artist picks up
a brush, dips it in paint and brings to life
a perky dog at the feet of the resident ghost,
companions forever in this foreign wood.

OLD MAN WITH A CANE

Fisheries Tower, Galway

He struggled across the bridge,
each step a creak,
to see the salmon jumping
and I wanted to call
to make fish leap
just for him.

It wasn't necessary;
his eyes weren't good.
He took vague shapes
in the Corrib for salmon,
saw the flash of silver as
they broke the surface.

CHESS GAME NEAR SLIGO

Closed in behind grey stone walls,
checkerboards of sheep and crows
spread out on either side of the road
strategy of field and woodlands.

Last traces of November leaves
form faded yellow arches,
scatter in the wind and drop,
loose piles in wet russet ditches.

I was not ready for Ben Bulben
or the poet's Isle of Inishfree,
the contours of Lough Gil winding,
enchantment suddenly upon me.

Through the damp constant drizzle,
soft noises of crows and sleepy sheep,
the existence of something good unseen,
definitely there, a feeling in the air.

DANCING AROUND SATURN

For Susan and Kevin, Galway

Cold fingers of the Atlantic
cannot quench the flame
that burns blue and amber
across chilly seas.

At Nimmo's Wine Bar,
three windows cut through
head, heart, and groin,
arranged in horizontal lines,
each revealing the night sky
with its stars ready to fall.

Projected like a film
a river runs so fast
it fades into grey-gold dots
as the sun slips drunkenly
behind a Claddagh skyline.

And there is life on Mars
seen in all its splendour,
life that is happy
in downpours and wet feet,
life that finds love
in a changeable climate.

Silent are the tongues,
resting before flight, wings whipping
loudly and rhythmically,
hungry for scraps,
scratching away in the Claddagh Basin
scribbling into the clouds.

We light a thousand candles,
throw back a glass of wine,
and open our arms to all of you
who can't stop smiling.
One deep breath, then another.

Music floats over Dominick Street.

CAPTURING THE ISLAND

Inismór, 19th Century*

Morning and painters come.
Seanín on the shore
scans the sky for weather,
still dark except for moonlight
on the whale back of the mainland,
the shadowy sea.

I wait alone
as he pulls off in his boat,
wait for him to join me again
over fields and mountains
to hear the birdsong,
stroke new-born calves,
the heat of sun on rocks.

Seanín, wrinkles line your face
etched by the North Atlantic
yet you keep a young man's eyes,
your special smile as I look out
at your boat of red petticoats, black shawl.

Maíre, your face smooth
like stones from the wind,
you standing as a beacon,
I sigh to see the black of your shawl,
the red of your petticoats.

Painters come
and they put us together,
another day at sea survived,
your red petticoats in port,
mine folded on a chair beside the bed.

* *Galway Hookers are wooden fishing and transport vessels with a black
form and red sails. The women of the island used to wear red skirts over
black petticoats.*

CORRIB

Galway

Herons live on the shore,
not here, said the American,
you'd see them back home
during the lobster season
when little grey boats
pulled into a weathered wharf.

But Galway herons nest
in someone's garden
in the busy city centre,
fish in the wild river
that brings in seals
and cormorants.

It is like rediscovering
a coelacanth,
extinct for hundreds of years,
or giving a mosquito a massage.

ADMITTANCE DENIED

Mount Jerome Cemetery, Dublin

No longer a grey city, but
this bleak November afternoon,
a ghost of the past whispers,
leaves crumple golden
under lifeless Dublin trees.

Your grey-haired son wants
to be with you on this day,
but, without flight, you are as distant
as the demoted planet Pluto.
A crow soars to where you rest.

At the gates in early darkness,
again a little boy left out,
sitting on the stairs in pajamas
to view a party where adults dance,
his cold-reddened hands shake
padlocked bars of iron.

Stones inside grow haphazardly
out of the dreary ground.

Locked out with old stories
going round in his head,
angry at the dusk closing
yet he's thankful not to be
locked in forever with the dead.

WAITING FOR THE LOCUSTS

Ireland's Celtic Tiger Years

I am like an elephant,
the one left to remember
but I have a bad memory
and am not afraid of mice.

We're going too fast,
everything whirls together,
I've been here for a long time,
as I said, an elephant.

Don't get me started
I was away in those times,
teaching English, courting in Irish
in the high middle of Spain.

But I know he *got done*,
we got roped in,
there's a rake of them
now, *getting done*.

And it's too late for us,
we let ourselves down,
we go through the motions,
wander into oblivion.

SOLITAIRE

Some people sit in cars,
there is one
outside my kitchen window
now as I make tea,
waiting, texting,
meditating, crying,
I watch and wonder
what they're doing.

It puts life into perspective,
you who wanted to fade
and flop into the void,
you who gave up the car,
cleaned out your closets,
made things simpler.

You thought you'd loosened the ties,
held the world at bay
but were tempted by bluebells,
first perfume of the season
and thought that waiting in cars
actually made sense,
made you realize what you were,

someone with a healthy appetite,
a taste for wine,
an attachment to the beauty
in this world
where manatees and dugongs
still swim in deep water.

BOREAL

UNDERWATER DREAMS

She sleeps,
breathing heavily,
in and out, in and out,
lullaby of her own making,
face a blank, suspended.

Calm surrounds,
deep in the deep,
she dreams of a sea
of tiny amethyst jelly fish,
pelagia noctiluca,
mauve stingers
and they are good.

A slight ruffling
as she changes colour
to match the pictures
that form within her lovely head.

In the muffled and murky
atmosphere
she goes chasing
vampire squid that drift past,
unaware.

Another change of colour,
she is in a different space
where echoes and hums
float towards her.

A crab stops a sideways journey
to burrow in sand
and comes to her dreams
as she breathes in and out, in and out,
and changes colour
one more time,
a reflex, a twitch to the eye,
a slight curling and flexing
of her eight powerful tentacles.

THE PLACE I DON'T GO

The mud river appeared and disappeared,
a tidal bore in a dull railway town,
grey city in sinking marsh
that encouraged mosquitos to multiply
and turned the bathwater brown.

Cruel of me to throw wet muck
against the fresh white wall,
this was a brand new home
for my mother and me,
we had to make it right.

My father lived somewhere else,
the place we lived before
where grey was hardly noticed
in the light clean air with the scent
of apple blossoms everywhere.

BURNT TOAST

Coming home from school,
the smell of burnt toast
signal that the lion has woken
and should be avoided at all costs.

Usually benign, eyes now flash,
sharp teeth are bared, a snarl
leaps at you who stands still,
praying the beast will tire and go.

It wanders off amongst the detritus
of empty rye whisky bottles,
neglecting to pull up its stockings
looking for a lair in which to sleep.

You've got off lightly this time,
no need to hide friends, barricade
the door, sleep in a snowbank.
Tomorrow sun and breakfast in bed.

THE WILD RIVER

He did well on the river
with ships up to the wharf
in back of his fine goods store,
carrying fashions from London,
linen shirts from Belfast,
oily wool from Scotland,
fine muslin from India.

He married well,
bought out Sutherland,
bought up land,
invested wisely.

He had a soft accent,
never mentioned home
to his nine children
only sharing a *cúpla focail* *
with his friend from Clare
over a sentimental whiskey
in his locked after-hours office.

He was remembered
in his homeland, the soft bog
of East Galway.

Yes, said his cousin Martin,
he was the only one gone 'way
that never sent back a penny.
He recalled it differently.
They never stopped fighting. He
visited home once, stayed away.

* a few words (in Irish Gaelic)

PEONIES

He didn't seem a man for flowers.
Behind the wheel of his black
1963 Chevrolet Bel Air,
in his dark suit and felt hat,
he'd make his way downriver
and bargain for horse manure
to enrich poor Maritime soil
to support a ritual passed on
from his Irish father to tend
peony roses, originally from China,
their fragrance nearly too luscious
for a rough new land of forest and sea:
yet worth it on the opening of blooms,
the palest pink, the deepest wine.

His wife was more for native flowers,
the simpler Indian Paintbrush, Brown-Eyed
Susans. She let him show off his gaudy ladies
yet whispered curses at petals that stained
the good table, and at ants that spilled out
the centres and marched to *God knows where*.

EATING STORIES

Only when the bay was frozen, snow lying
five-foot deep and icicles hanging as big as
your arm, did he realize he hadn't been paid.
His wife dreamt of a new coat,
He's a nice man but we can't wear stories.

It was their way to cut firewood
and pile it ready for the cold,
to have a freezer full of vegetables
from the summer garden, meat from
a moose shot in hunting season, fish,
lobster, crab, mussels they caught,
pickles, jams, and jellies in the cupboard
so no one will freeze or starve.

When sap flows from trees into buckets,
boils in cauldrons, hardens on snow,
winter-weighted boughs get lighter,
ice cracks in the bay, flows out to sea,
a time to take off the cottage shutters,
turn on the water mains, the electricity,
and to shyly ask for what is owed.

But with tales stored in his head
throughout the New Brunswick cold,
the old man asks him in,
presses a whiskey in his hand
and captivates him once more.

PIECES OF THE PUZZLE

My face, she said, looked like
it belonged in a cottage by the sea,
a face that looked at home on every street,
one that got asked directions in Havana
from a Cuban woman in from the country,
acknowledged in Paris by an elegant woman
with two coiffed poodles,
or a plea for help from
a destitute German in Madrid,
language no barrier.

Often unnoticed, always familiar
but not at home,
a face like a sandstone,
sand and stone, full of holes
eroding, shifting, reforming

until the face reflected in the mirror
becomes the face of a person
who lives in a cottage by the sea.

TORNADO WARNING

Nebraska

Lincoln morning, cold presence
of military on streets,
remnants of snow on pavement,
a white jigsaw puzzle.

Americans of the plains
and Norwegian settlers
stare out from photographs
at the Nebraska History Museum
among exquisite artifacts.

What have we done to each other?
Msit No'Kmaq
All our ancestors
No separation
smoked a peace pipe
smoked a peace pipe
smoked a pipe, peace.

In the afternoon, leaving,
an airport official frisks
passengers,
then waves us through,

past the tornado tunnel,
a sanctuary, the only shelter,
though too late –
the plane caught
like a bug in a vortex.

Smoked a peace pipe.

RETURN FLIGHT/
AS THE CROW FLIES

AIR FORCE BLUE

Operation Blue Skies, 1953

His/her birth was in a foreign country,
the year they learned to change
weather from blue skies to veils
of mist and charcoal grey,
conditions confusing for crows,
strange happenings deep under
mountains, warm hall of trolls.

He/she would like to explore more
but the weather in his/her head
is cloudy and shows signs of
severe thunderstorms - a warning
to unplug radios and televisions,
stay away from sinks, and metal pipes.
Leave the laundry on the clothesline
and if outdoors, take shelter in a ditch,
Never, never, go under a tree.

Wise to stay away from mountains too.

RAVENSCRAG

Montreal, 1959

The solemn stone house on the hill
pulled me to it as if I had been before
but it was my mother entertained there
in induced slumber, interrupted sleep,
played-back words and suggestions,
truth serum and LSD testing
before the days of flower children.

Then, cured, back to an old life,
triggers hidden, but she was never the same,
ravens always waiting on the outside branch
to whisk her back up the hill.

Why, when weak and searching a hospital,
did I pass through those doors,
walk empty corridors, suddenly
to realize my mistake, and feel the chill?

CITY INFRASTRUCTURE

Ley lines lead down to the river
where water leaps and leaves frolic,
restless hearts lifted into the air
evading a spotlight searching stars.

Water bruises, scaffolding tumbles,
cement cracks, wrecking bridges,
winter dirt and branches cover cars
held together by rusty scraps of metal.

Fog drifts away from the *St. Laurent*
for clear vision across to the shore
yet no longer can the signs be read
of a life left behind on the mainland.

The mountain in the middle rests,
a heavy-eyed volcano, long dormant,
dreaming of animals scampering in trees,
glittering towers wake to perform below.

MONTREAL'S SWING INTO SPRING

Snow lingers like dirty lingerie on cement,
wind prowls the theatre district and pounces
on mufflered students on the walk uphill to class.

The swings were put up late this year,
supposed to be a one-off installation,
now an annual event,
fun for *les montréalais* and tourists alike
and so welcome after a long cold winter.

Six in a row, they sing with different notes
to create a coordinated sweet melody
yet silent when not pushed up and down.

I join in a tune, going higher and higher,
laughing like a child but sad because you
are no longer there when I shout *Look at Me.*

TONGUE TIED IN MONTREAL

after Mark Abley

Wind whispers in two languages,
trees dance in their new colours,
my wrought iron bed stands
on a Quebec wooden floor.

In my sleep I speak a magical *Irish*,
the room quakes and trills with its beauty,
I am back along the canals of Galway,
the language rising from water as spray.

By the end of this century
half of the seven thousand
tongues now spoken will be silent,
some leave behind a few scrawled signs,
others, no trace,
a people, a culture vanish.

A language, once moribund,
will no longer sing in the mouths
of those it meant something to,
leaving academics to record the last speaker
after a tribe is wiped out,
transcribe words from a parrot.

In Quebec, I try French and English.
I squawk, let words out of a container,
do my best and sometimes it is enough.

I wake, the taste of watermelon on my tongue.

LITTLE POOLS OF LIGHT

after Leonard Cohen's *A Hundred Kisses Deep*

Sheep then leap to bring on sleep,
the fences are too high.
you shut your eyes and cease to weep,
a simple lullaby,

and on a dark and lonely breeze,
gliding bats begin to fright,
wild eyes look at you from trees.
little pools of light.

The worm is hidden in the fruit,
crows stab with their beaks,
the apple sticks, makes them mute.
a circus act of freaks.

Back and forth the crash of waves,
decide what you can keep,
chambered in the mind, it rests
in the place of good sleeps.

But what waits out in the forest dark
or through your inner sight,
by the sea or in the park?
Little pools of light.

Go deep down and meet the child
and ask it what it wants,
it's standing in a river mild,
frightened, small, and gaunt.

Look at that one and take its hand,
you recognize its plight,
walk with it in that murky land
to find little pools of light.

ACKNOWLEDGEMENTS

Some of these poems have been published in some form in Qwerty, Fusion, iota, Crannóg, The Prairie Schooner, Stony Thursday, Exposed, Irlandesas, West 47, Revival, Artistic Atlas of Galway, NB Shamrock, White Chimney, Blinkzone, Tribe Vibes. *Dogs Singing* anthology by Salmon.

BIO

Sandra Bunting writes poetry, fiction, non-fiction, and journalistic articles. Her first poetry collection, *Identified In Trees,* Marram Press, was followed by a chapbook, *Lake of Phantoms* by Mercutio Press, Montreal. Her collection of short stories, *The Effect Of Frost On Southern Vines,* was published in 2016, her second, *Everything in this House Breaks,* in 2018.

She grew up in northern New Brunswick and was awarded a BA in Radio and Television Arts from Toronto Metropolitan University and an MA in Writing from the University of Galway, Ireland. After working for CBC News, Toronto, she moved to Europe and lived in the north of France, Madrid, Dublin, and Galway. She returned to Canada in 2011.

Sandra is currently on the editorial board of the Galway-based literary magazine, *Crannóg,* and works at Gaelóg Press, which offers writing and editing services, and creative writing workshops.

In her academic career, Sandra facilitated creative writing classes at the University of Galway, where she also set up and managed the Academic Writing Centre. She taught English as a Second Language and was involved in EFL Teacher Training.

In 2012 she was awarded a Glenna Luschei award for poetry through the 'Prairie Schooner', University of Nebraska. She was runner-up for the 2006 Welsh Cinnamon Press First Novel Competition and was a finalist at the 2009 Irish Digital Media Awards for her Blog: *Writing a Novel Online.*

Sandra's work has appeared widely in literary journals in Canada, the US, the UK, and Ireland. This is Sandra's third poetry collection, and you can find more information on her work, and Gaelóg Press at:

www.sandbunting.com

Gaelóg Press